Prolance

www.prolancewriting.com
California, USA
©2017 Ayesha Desai
Cover art ©2017 Jenny Reynish

All rights reserved. No part of the publication may be reproduced in any form without prior permission from the publisher.

ISBN: 978-0-9983287-6-8

Jasmine in the Wind

Written by Ayesha Desai
Cover art by Jenny Reynish

PROLANCE

This work is dedicated to my parents, for your undying love and support and your constant prayers for my success. Thank you for being the first people who believed in me, and helping me to believe in myself.

To my sisters (biological, by marriage, by soul). The ladies who have my back, who laugh with me, cry with me, hold me up, cheer me on, and straight talk. Thank you for your friendship, and honesty.

To my husband, my biggest supporter, my number one fan. Without you by my side, I would never be able to accomplish half the things that I have in my life. Thank you for being my best friend, my critic, my confidante, my life coach, my partner in life.

To my children, Mohamed Zakir and Ridaa. This book was written to show you that any obstacle can be overcome, that your life potential is truly limitless, and that dreams do come true.

Most importantly, to the children of Syria, and every war-torn land. Your displays of bravery and courage leave me in amazement. Your strength of character, and heart are astounding. You have seen and lived through what no child ever should, and I can only pray that future generations of children never have to. This is your story and the world owes you the greatest apology. I continue to live in hope that one day love will rule, justice will reign and peace will return.

Freedom Drowns

When this world confuses and confounds you
And when the uncertainty surrounds you
Whilst other people sleep
And you and yours weep
When mistrust abounds
And in fear, freedom drowns
When the ocean beckons
But death appears in second.

Disclaimer

This story and the characters herein are entirely fictitious. Certain events, and places are mentioned, and whilst inspiration was drawn from current events the author has used a liberal dose of artistic license to create the characters and narrative of the story which is wholly imaginary. Any resemblance to actual persons, living or dead, and/or names of characters, is purely coincidental.

Jasmine in the Wind

Afraa's legs ached and her muscles cramped as she continued to walk. The broken strap on the sandals she wore made it even more difficult to keep putting one foot in front of the other. She bent down, removed her shoes and tucked them into her pocket and was thinking about walking barefoot, but quickly realized that the tar on the road was too hot. It burnt her feet, so she put her broken sandal back on. Afraa tried concentrating on walking on the white line that ran down the center of the road.

She needed to focus on anything besides the burning pain in her calf muscles. The hordes of people around her were just not cooperating with her unvoiced request to stop pushing and shoving. Last night the road had looked like an unending suede ribbon sprinkled with glittering lights but today, in this heat and desperation, it was littered with a great crush of people. There was nothing to be done but keep moving with this surging river, to contend with the claustrophobia as the highway took on a life of its own.

Sometimes a child or an elderly person would stumble, but carrying the young was not an option. Taking a break and allowing the elderly to rest wasn't an option either. Every able bodied person and most of the children too, were laden with the odd assortment of bags and memories and supplies they could possibly haul.

As usual to combat that rising bile of fear, Afraa started an imaginary conversation with her best friend Nadiha, about the unruliness of the others walking the same path. Nadiha understood. Nadiha always understood Afraa's heart. "Yallah, Afraa, come," Mama interrupted their conversation as she beckoned for Afraa to hurry up. There were hundreds of people around them and she didn't want to get lost in this crowd.

There was a murmur in the crowd. Afraa looked up to see the exhausted faces around her start talking excitedly. And then peoples voices and hands soared up like they wished to touch the sky itself, like salvation and deliverance was raining down.

She heard the words water, fruit, bread, and people

seemed to have found a new energy from some secret storage place. Afraa stayed close to her family, she didn't know what was happening.

There was no time to continue the conversation with Nadiha now. People were shouting now, "Please, we have children with us. Another bottle of water please!" It was Baba. He handed her a bottle of water and said, "Put this in your bag." Afraa yanked her backpack off her shoulders and struggled clumsily with the zip. She had no energy to navigate it, and so her dad took it from her hands, hurriedly placed two bottles of water into it, and put the straps of the backpack onto her shoulders again. Then he picked up the loaf of bread he had placed at her feet, tore off a chunk of bread, handed a piece to her, then one to her mother and one for her baby brother. There wasn't more than a mouthful left for him, but all he seemed to care about was making sure his family ate.

Afraa blew the dust off the bread, and gingerly lifted it to her lips. The bread was soft, and fresh, but it was dry. Afraa wished she had just a little drop of honey to sweeten it. She didn't realize how hungry she had been until she bit off a mouthful. Her mouth was dry and it was hard to chew and even harder to swallow. Her throat felt drier than the baked summer earth. Afraa realized that she had never truly been thirsty before this journey began. There had always been something to drink, refreshing chilled water, sparkling cool juices, with ice blocks dancing in the colorful plastic jugs.

Intricately decorated teapots of richly flavored and aromatic teas were constantly refilled on little side tables.

Never once had she drank to quench her discomfort. But now just plain water was like the greatest luxury on earth. She gulped down the water Mama had given her. It rushed down her throat and happily filled her stomach.

There was another group of people walking amongst them now, handing out more water, apples, oranges, diapers for babies. These were people whose clothes weren't dusty, and their faces didn't look exhausted. They were clean, and there were no tear streaks down their cheeks, their hair didn't have that ragged steel wool look caused by ocean water. "Look Mama, shoes!" she said as she pointed to a man with wild red hair and glasses. He was sitting next to shopping cart filled with shoes, and handing them out to people as they asked. Afraa's mom grabbed her hand and they made their way to the man. Afraa's mom pointed to her broken shoe and said, "Shabbat." He smiled, and said something kindly. Well, Afraa didn't know for sure it if was something kindly but he had kind eyes, and handed over a pair of blue sneakers. They were obviously meant for boys but Afraa didn't care. It was better than walking in broken shoes. It felt like they had been walking for days, and who knew how much further they had to go. Afraa sat on the ground and tried on the shoe, it was slightly big, but her feet already felt better. As her mother thanked him, "Shukron," he motioned for them to wait, and then handed over two pairs

Jasmine in the Wind

of socks for her, and seeing her little brother, he also gave them what looked like two fluffy bears, but as she looked closer, Afraa saw that it was in fact a pair of slippers.

"Dalia, Afraa, Yahya," she heard her father shout above the hustle and bustle. "The train, it's here. Ta'aal. Hurry," as he dragged Mama, who dragged Afraa. They were squashed, and shoved, and pushed around as people fought to get onto the train. Mama was yanked away from Afraa, there were people shouting, Afraa screamed, "Mama, Mama," when suddenly strong hands were around her waist and she was being lifted in the air. She screamed even louder, and then was suddenly through the entryway, and placed on her feet. She turned around to see that it was her Abdo Yassin- Mama's younger brother, who had left two weeks before they did.

Afraa hugged him tightly, and then so did Mama and Baba. "Afraa habibi, you must stay close." Afraa nodded, overwhelmed and relieved and barely able to keep her eyes open. When the train finally splutters to life, it brings a strange cocktail of feelings, some relief, some fear, some grieving for the place they left, some sorrow for the paths they've walked, some regret for the choices they've made, and as always it seems, a generous helping of anxiety. Ahead is the unknown, and all they can do is pray for things to be better where they are heading, but all they know of it is what they've heard, and now experience has taught them that the frenzied, frantic need to escape pain often peppered hearsay with an overdose of optimism. Some passengers cry, some look stoic, and the children are held close and comforted with words the parents pray are not empty promises.

Afraa looked out the window and then back at her family. Her baby brother was laying on Baba's lap, and Mama gently took Afraa into her arms now, and laid her head on her own lap. It wasn't the most comfortable place to sleep, but it was certainly better than sleeping in the tall grasses as they did last night...or maybe it was the night before. This whole horrid journey had meshed into one long nightmare now. Then they had a piece of cardboard, and she and Yahya lay down on that. Her parents slept sitting up against a tree trunk. It was cold and noisy, and her ears hurt. Yahya either cried a lot, or just slipped into a silent wait, for what hardship was to come next.

Soon the rocking motion of the train and the gentle hum of its desperate passengers allowed her to drift off. Suddenly she felt like she was below the water again, holding her breath, kicking, Baba screaming for her to stop thrashing about so he could pull her back up. She remembered all too vividly how they were squeezed into the small plastic boat. Baba had insisted they be given life jackets but there was only two, and so it went to Mama and another lady who was pregnant. Afraa had sat next to Baba, but then a great wave rose high above them and sent the little boat bouncing about like one of the bouncing balls she used to own. Then it settled, and the smelly smuggler man warned them not to scream or the coastguard would be alerted, they would arrest them and send them all back home.

The next moment there was another giant tower of water above them and Afraa and a boy she had known from school, Khaled, were suddenly in the freezing water. It stung her eyes, and burnt her throat. Both of them were pulled back on-board but their families were furious! The smuggler didn't care, and asked, "Want me to turn boat around?" The other children huddled down between their parents, and the only sounds were that of the water and whispered prayers. When they eventually sighted land, the smuggler jumped into the water and swam away to an awaiting speedboat. Baba and the other men tried getting close to the shore, then got into the water and pulled the boat ashore.

Afraa had assumed this was it! They made it. She thought this was end of the journey...but it had been only the beginning. "Afraa, Afraa," she heard Mama shout desperately. She opened her eyes, and was blanketed in confusion, before she remembered that she was on the train. "The water Mama, it was cold, and I was under and I couldn't breathe..."

"I was passing Mama a bottle of water and a few droplets fell on your forehead," said Baba.

"You're ok, baby. We're almost there, we're going to be safe...I promise you," he said as he hugged her.

The train rolled on, but Afraa couldn't sleep anymore. She looked at her father's face, there were lines there that weren't there before. His hair had more grey in it, the stubble on his cheeks made him look tired. Mama's hands were shaking, they shook all the time now, and her eyes were sunken and darker somehow. Even little Yayha wasn't the ball of nonsense he usually was. He was only ever this quiet and this still, when the sirens started blaring, and soon after the jets would fly over. Afraa would tremble at the sound of it, but Yahya would just sit still and listen, until the ground started shaking. Everyone in the train was quiet now, the exhaustion seemed to have cocooned them in silence.

Afraa thought back to that last jet, the one that had sent a bomb smashing through Abdo Reeza's house. She remembered the ground shaking, the sirens screaming, and that sudden whooshing sound that hurt her ears, and then the crashing sound as the bomb hit a part of the house. The air was thick with smoke and dust and every breath ached. Little Yahya looked like he wanted to cry but couldn't do much, and so silent tears streamed down his face. They turned around to look once more, and there was only rubble. Afraa wanted so much to turn around and run back into the compound, to look for Abdo Reeza, but in her hearts of hearts she knew that the hug she had only hours earlier shared with him, would be the last. Mama was crying silently as they crouched closer to the ground, and they searched for the tunnel they knew wasn't far off. Just as the blaring sirens got closer, and the soldier's screams were heard, Baba found it and motioned for Mama to enter, and then Afraa followed, while Baba had Yahya tied to him.

They crawled and crouched for what seemed like hours, and Afraa's hands were scratched and aching, but eventually that too became numb. Abdo Reeza was no more. Her home was no more. Where were they even going? Afraa had no idea, but knew that danger was at every step. Her pounding heart, now shattered again, for the hundredth time in such a short lifespan, kept hammering against her ribs. The air in the tunnel was stale, and dry, and Afraa thought she was going to pass out a few times. Yahya, she was sure was already unconscious. Eventually they saw a light in the darkness, flashing once, then twice, then nothing for two minutes, then the signal again. Mama hesitated. Baba squeezed through passed them both, and exited the tunnel. Afraa heard voices on the outside, and then Baba came back for them.

"Quick, rush, it's almost daylight, we don't have much time!" he whispered. They scrambled out of the hole in the ground, and were quickly herded into an awaiting lorry. There were other people too. Even a family who lived just a few roads away from where Afraa did. Khaled a boy who was in her class was amongst the terrified ones sitting and shivering in the back of the cold lorry. About fifteen minutes later, another couple joined them, the lady was heavily pregnant, and her face red with exhaustion. She and her husband were young, and from the scars and bruises on his face and the ugly limp with which he walked, you could tell they had an even harder time getting here.

Once everyone was stuffed into the lorry, they were given strict instructions to keep the children quiet, to be absolutely still, and above all else to pray!

The lorry was loaded with crates of nuts and sugar beets, and soon the little air in there disappeared. It was absolutely black, and through it all Yahya never made a single sound. Afraa on the other hand, wanted to scream, but there was no scream loud enough to shout her pain and fear. The lorry rolled on for hours, through bumpy roads, and stopped intermittently where they would hear shouts, and machine guns, and men screaming, and once a woman's scream so horrifying the sound kept ringing in Afraa's ears long after they had driven off. She gripped onto Mama's hand, who reassuringly squeezed hers back. One of the baby's started crying and everyone held their breath in anticipation of finding themselves at the end of one of those machine guns they heard every couple of hours.

Suddenly the lorry stopped, and the doors were opened, and the rush of fresh air had everyone gasping. "You, you, ta'aal, come, now, run. Follow Majid here, be quick! Move, move." The man pointed at Baba, and at Khaled's father. Both men grabbed their families and jumped out. Afraa's legs were stiff, and cramping, and she desperately needed to go to the toilet, not to mention the fact that her throat was so dry, her tongue felt heavy. The lorry quickly started up again, and rushed off in the opposite direction from where it came. They followed the man named Majid into the forest, the sticks cut into her legs, but the urgency and desperation made them keep running. Eventually they were at what Majid said was the border. The fence was cut, and he held it apart, and said, "This is as far as I take you. Go, be quiet, and stay close to the ground. Stay close to the bushes so the soldiers don't see you. And pray!"

He said this, as he handed them a bag of food, and ran off into the darkness. The two families decided to stick together, and rest for a while, and that was when Afraa crumpled like a puppeteer suddenly released of her strings. Her mind was swirling, and the darkness of the world around her captured her completely as it all turned black. She felt like she slept for years. When she woke, she found herself on her Baba's back, as he moved quietly. Everything from that point on, was a blur to Afraa. Her dreams were peppered with images of her and Nadiha, playing dress up with their moms hijabs, and then being chased by runaway lorries, and Nadiha disappearing and Jiddoh and Abdo Reeza digging tunnels for them, and tornadoes which rained down sweet tea! Afraa's little body was exhausted, but so was her heart and mind. She kept seeing Abdo Reeza's house collapse in front of her. She imagined him sometimes being asleep knowing they were about to leave and being at peace about it, and so the bomb didn't hurt him, and he died in his sleep. Other times, she imagined him, watching them from his window, making sure that they left safely, and then she saw his happy face being smashed, and had images of blood and horror in her little mind, that should never be in the mind of a child. How she had loved the old man, her grandfather's best friend, her second grandfather!

Abdo Reeza and his wife Amto Samia were their next door neighbors. All of their children and grandchildren had left a few months ago on the back of a truck. Abdo Reeza and Afraa's grandfather, her Jiddoh Yousef, had been friends since they were little boys. Their two houses had a shared courtyard now, and both old men had lost their wives. They had now only their children and grandchildren and memories of times gone by. Jiddoh and Abdo Reeza would sit outside under the ancient pomegranate tree, and sip mint tea, fondly remember the past, sharing their stories with their grandchildren.

Afraa's favorite stories were about the tourists who would visit Damascus to see the great Umayyad mosque there. Afraa had been there once, and remembered walking through the cobbled alleyways, and passed the collapsing Greek columns, and entering that great courtyard. The cool marble, the beautiful mosaics high up that she had first thought were paintings, the soft red carpets inside the mosque, the towering minarets, were all so beautiful and magical and mystical. She remembered being amazed by the tomb of Nabi Yahya inside the mosque and the many of tourists, even those who were not Muslim, visiting it. Later that evening Baba had taken them to a restaurant at a fancy tourist hotel in Sayyidah Zeinab suburb, and they dined on Fattoush and Freekeh with lamb. Fattoush is a crunchy salad with chunky bits of tomatoes, cucumber, radish, and thin pieces of baked bread to soak up the sharply flavored dressing. Freekeh is a green wheat pilaf dish with peas, pine nuts, almonds, butter and spices. And then they had Mhalabia which is a delicious milky pudding with coconut and pistachio as a special treat. Mama usually only made it on special occasions. It was some of Afraa's favorite dishes.

It was a wonderful day that Afraa often thought back on with a smile...But when her Jiddoh Yousef and Abdo Reeza spoke of Damascus, it was when they were the young ones, selling pomegranates, and roasted corn on the cob to the tourists, or helping them carry their bags and luggage into the hotels, or even carrying their shopping when they visited the bustling souks, and museums and palaces. They spoke of stories of their boyhood holidays to Al Samra beach, and the ancient ruins of Palmyra just north of Damascus. Teta's family was from Aleppo, and Jiddoh often spoke of the time he and Teta visited the great citadel there just after they married. Teta died when Afraa was just a tiny baby, but the beautiful tapestry she did still adorned the walls of the house. Afraa often stared at those tiny intricate stitches and imagined her grandmother choosing the colors to bring the artwork to life. Afraa missed the stories.

When Jiddoh passed away, Abdo Reeza promised Afraa that for as long as he was alive, he would be her Jiddoh, and he would love her as loved all of his many grandchildren. But now nobody sat outside and spoke anymore, it was too dangerous. Everything was too dangerous now! The rubble-strewn streets, and constant blaring sirens, and broken people and broken hearts made that Syria seem so long ago.

That's why all of Abdo Reeza's family had left. He made them leave, saying he hadn't worked so hard all his life just to bury his children one after the other. His daughter Rania had already passed away, and he wasn't going to lose any more of his children, so he made them leave. Afraa missed them, especially her friend Nadiha, they were the only two girls amongst the whole group of boys.

Afraa wondered would she ever be able to go back to Syria. Would there be anything to go back to? Did she even want to go back? Would she remember what her house looked like? Would she would ever see Nadiha again?

So many thoughts running through her mind...On one hand she never wanted to forget her homeland, her Syria! On the other hand, there were so many things, she wished she wouldn't remember.

Like the day the soldiers came knocking on their

doors, late at night. Afraa was just getting into bed, and they were made to stand outside their house in the cold, whilst the soldiers searched their home. There was nothing there, but still they took Baba away. Mama was too scared to stay in the house and started making plans to go to her family in Jordan, but then the soldiers came back the next day, and left Baba at the gate. He said they were watching the house, and we couldn't leave, so we carried on trying to live as normally as we could...but that was the starting point. The day everything changed!

A few days later, Abdo Reeza's sons came to visit Baba one night. Afraa was supposed to be in bed, but couldn't resist standing in the shadows listening. She squashed herself into the corner and stretched her ears. Afraa was always getting into trouble for listening in on adults conversations but this time the air tingled with ideas so much that she really needed to know. They were trying to convince Baba to leave with them. He said we didn't have enough money for the trip, they should take their families and leave while they still can, and he would try to find some resources. The very next day, on the way to school, Afraa, Nadiha, and two other girls, were stopped by the soldiers.

They were made to empty their bags, and sit on the pavement. They missed school that day. They were thirsty and hungry, and the soldiers were terrifying. They stopped more schoolgirls throughout the day. All the children were made to empty their schoolbags, and simply sit there in the sun.

When they didn't return home after school, their fathers and uncles and brothers went out searching for the girls, and once located by their families, the girls were allowed to go home on condition that the men stayed behind to join the fighting. One of the men refused to let his teenage son stay behind, and offered to stay himself instead.

The soldiers didn't like his arguing, and so shot him, right there, in front of everyone. Afraa and Nadiha screamed, and the guns were quickly aimed at them. The girl whose father had been shot, just stared at her father laying there, as his eyes rolled up, and a pool of blood leaked out of his head. Her brother shouted and shouted, and screamed, and was suddenly butted in his face with the end of a gun. He too fell to the ground in a heap. It was the first time, Afraa had seen such horror, and knew that she would never forget that empty look in the man's eyes as his soul floated away.

Baba and Nadiha's father quickly realized that there were no arguments to be made, and opted to stay, on condition that the girls be allowed to leave immediately. For the second time that week, Baba had been taken away. Afraa never went to school again, after that day. Mama was frantic when one day turned to two, then a week, then a month, and there was no sign of Baba. Mama spent every night praying and keeping watch at the windows. The sounds of gunfire were constant these days, as were the sounds of mothers crying as their husbands and sons were taken from their homes in the darkness of night.

Afraa remembered overhearing another conversation where the adults didn't even know of which group the fighters belonged to. Were they government soldiers, or rebels, nobody knew. It didn't even matter. They terrified the people regardless. Abdo Reeza said his family would take Mama, Yahya and me with them. Nadiha's father Hussein had been sent back two weeks ago, and their plans to leave were now set. Abdo Reeza had spent many hours in the last week, writing down details and stories of his family history for his grandchildren to take with them. He whispered prayers, and stole hugs, and kissed foreheads every chance he got, and hurriedly wiped the tears out of his eyes with the corner of his red and white checkered Shumaq scarf that always sat comfortably atop his head. But he refused to leave, saying he was an old man, and Syria was in his veins. He wanted to die here, but he would die happy knowing his family was starting over in a new place, in a safe place.

Abdo Yassin, Mama's brother came to visit one night, he brought sweets with for Afraa, and medicines for Mama. He said he had seen Baba, and he was ok. That was when Mama decided that she couldn't leave, she wouldn't leave without Baba. Abdo Yassin said he was working on a plan, that would get us to Turkey, and that we'd go as soon as Baba was home.

He needed money to pay some people, who would give it to others, and help us sneak out of the only place we'd ever known. Mama gave him a gold coin that had been her mehr, her wedding dowry, and a little bit of jewelery she had left. Just before leaving Abdo Yassin, told Mama to pack a bag, and keep it hidden. That night Mama and I packed half the medicine that Abdo Yassin brought into a bag, packets of crackers, some peanuts, t-shirts and underwear for us, and diapers for Yahya, a few photographs, a phone charger, and some money.

Then she packed another bag with the exact identical contents. Over the next few days, Mama found copies of my school reports, and mine and Yahya's birth certificates, and wrapped them in separate plastic bags, and added this to each of the backpacks. We hugged and prayed for Abdo Reeza's family as they snuck out of the house, two or 3 of them at a time over the last week. We gave our extra food and blankets to Abdo Reeza, and slowly and quietly Mama started selling off the other things in the house.

The last thing to go was the TV that Baba had been so proud of when he brought it home. He'd received it as a present from his students at the end of the year. Afraa almost hadn't recognized Um Ahmad when she came to pay for the TV. Um Ahmad had been a chubby, permanently smiley lady who sold delicious traditional goodies like baklawa and Syrian

cigar Pastries from home. Her husband had died years earlier in a bus collision when the family were returning from a visit to Norias of Hama. Afraa learnt about these water wheels in a history lesson at school and once upon a time
really wanted to see them.

Since then Um Ahmad made a living by becoming a well known confectioner. Afraa remembered the long queues outside Um Ahmad's home in the evenings of Ramadan as she and Nadiha waited to buy baklawa for the family to enjoy after their fast for the day. For a moment she closed her eyes and imagined the sizzle of the hot syrup as it was poured over the thin flaky pastry. She used to run home with her bag of goodies, Nadiha with bright green eyes brimming with excitement running at her side, as they anticipated the first bite of the golden deliciousness. Mama always kept a few of the cigar Pastries aside for Baba to enjoy after the Taraweeh prayer. It was filled with a delicious orange honey cream. For a fraction of a second Afraa almost ran her tongue over her lips remembering the taste and then the thundering sound of a truck raced by and Afraa was jolted back to the present…where Um Ahmad was now a frightfully thin lady who's eyes darted about nervously as she explained to Mama why she wanted the television set.

Her son Ahmad who at the beginning of the horror was set to become a doctor and was planning on going to study at a college in London. He'd studied really hard and had achieved great results and got a bursary. Afraa remembered a newspaper article about him and how proud Jiddoh and Abdo Reeza were of this young boy who had grown up carrying parcels of pastries about the neighborhood and the possibility of him amounting to so much more. They were more proud because of Baba's association to him. Ahmad had been one of Baba's most promising students. Nadiha's brothers grew tired of hearing about amazing Ahmad.

Back then there wasn't any actual fighting yet, just lots of tension and many demonstrations. Ahmad, who was also a keen photographer, went to one of the big rallies, and was taking pictures of the crowds, when a stray bullet that had been fired into the air landed in his back! Ahmad was in hospital for a long time, and at one stage there had been hope of a recovery after the bullet was removed. Then the fighting got worse, and the hospital couldn't keep him any longer as their beds quickly filled up and their resources quickly emptied out. Um Ahmad couldn't afford the physiotherapy, and Ahmad was now a paraplegic confined to his wheelchair. A TV would be the last chance for Um Ahmad to show her son with the big dreams a small glimpse of the outside world. The promise of his success had whispered enchantingly, like darkness surrendering to the light. Life for him was supposed to be full of possibility, freshness and newness to come. Now it sat like a stale pile of khubz bread waiting to be crushed into crumbs and scattered to the birds.

Jasmine in the Wind

Mama said she would pray for them both always, and gave Um Ahmad an old jacket that Baba no longer wore. The cold winter winds were already sighing as they settled in to stay. The price of basic necessities were very high now, and Mama knew that Um Ahmad wouldn't be able to provide much heat for their home. In this small way, Ahmad would still have a small measure of the warmth of his old school teacher. Then after Um Ahmad left, Mama made sure to divide the money equally between the two backpacks. Whenever Afraa asked her why she was doing that, her answer was always the same, "You never know Afraa. You can never be too careful." Now, Afraa knew she meant that if either one of her parents, hadn't survived this journey, then at least the other wouldn't be completely stranded, and without money.

Just a few days later, there was a knock on the compound door, and as usual Mama motioned for me, to push the great chair over the hole in the floor we had dug, and hidden the bags in. The soldiers came searching at random times now. But that night...it was Baba! He was thin and dirty, and had no shoes, and there was now an ugly angry scar that ran from his hairline down just past his left eyebrow, but he was back. Abdo Reeza insisted we leave as soon as Baba was strong enough to travel. Abdo Yassin had already made all the arrangements before he left. Through all the horror that Afraa had seen, she had never shed a tear, but that night Afraa cried when she hugged Abdo Reeza for the very last time! And that's how she came to be, here, now, sitting on this train. Eventually the rolling stopped, and they were greeted by more pale smiling faces, and people trying to speak Arabic, "Marhaba, marhaba ala Deutschland."

"Deutschland?" Afraa asked her dad. He nodded, and smiled. "It's over habibi, we're here, this is going to be home, you're going to be safe! No more bombs, no more soldiers, no more hunger!"

Her mom's eyes were full of tears, and Abdo Yassin had a goofy grin on his face. Afraa wanted to join in with the happy celebrations, like so many of the other adults around them, but the children, like Afraa just looked tired, and confused, and unsure.

How can this place be home?

Home is across the land, across the ocean, a bleeding soil. But...Home is broken...so maybe, maybe they could build a new home here, in this place called Deutschland, this Germany!

This place of strange language, and strange dress, where people eat pork, and have blue eyes, the likes of which Afraa had never seen before. They were taken to what looked like a school, and into a large hall that already had many families there. They were then directed to a spot in the corner, where there were two mattresses on the floor, and a blanket.

Jasmine in the Wind

Baba had to go with the policemen to fill in papers, and when Mama reached for the passports and birth certificates, they were now crumpled from when the bags got wet in the small rubber boat. But still, they had all of their papers, and were told that it would be quicker to find them a place to stay because of it, and because both Mama and Baba had studied and had university degrees. That was when Afraa decided that no matter what happened, she would study hard, and make sure she got a university degree too! Mama was allowed to call her brother in Jordan and tell him that we were safe now, and the process for staying here permanently had begun.

Staying in the hall was difficult, the place was crowded, and the bathrooms inadequate. But as more people came through the doorways and they heard more stories of other horrors in the refugee camps, and border closures, and assaults by the locals, Afraa made peace with the fact that there was no rewind button to the last few years of her life. There would be no more imaginary conversations with Nadiha now. They had learnt a few days ago that the boat Nadiha's family were on capsized in a storm. Nadiha and her younger brother never survived. Afraa's heart broke all over again. Nadiha's family were in the process of relocating to Canada. Nothing she'd seen would be forgotten, there was no eraser that would make her forget the pain, and yet she was still grateful that her family were together, that they had a chance to rebuild, that they were relatively healthy, and that their scars, physical and emotional would be healed.

Weeks passed and Afraa had started school now, a refugee school they called it, which was filled with children from Syria, but also Iraq, and Palestine, and people who were the exact opposite of the pale Germans. They were Kenyans, and Somalis and other people from Africa too. All these people with their different languages and colors, who could barely speak to each other had the same story. Stories that didn't need words. Stories that were conveyed and understood through the eyes, through the heart, through the spirit. Like the time Mama-Jamelah from Congo, was holding a small carved wooden keyring, and burst into tears, and Mama hugged her, and cried with her, both women speaking different languages but the same story of home, of horror, of determination, of struggles, of pain and loss, of hope, and longing. Mama-Jamelah they came to know was a brilliant cook, and soon volunteered to manage the kitchen, much to the delight of those in the center. Afraa's world was opening up, to different tastes and new ways of life.

The refugees lived in almost isolated colonies, where the pale people would come every day, bringing food, and medicines, and clothing. There were counselors too who spoke to the children kindly, and played games with them. Eventually they were given a place of their own, with their own bathroom! Families were placed before single people. The flat was sparse, with thin sponge mattresses on the floor, and a big plastic box for their clothing, a few kitchen items. There was a gauzy net curtain that displayed patterns on the wall when the sun shone. Baba had gotten work, not as teacher, but as a builder, and each night he came back to the tiny flat with rough hands and splinters in his fingers. And on weekends, he worked at a factory, loading and unloading boxes from large trucks. Baba was proud of his work, proud that he could support us and pay back the kindness of the people. The children were now all trying to twist their tongues to this newly found common language they were taught at school. It was a unifying factor, amongst the children in the colony, and slowly the languages and games and food were merging one into another. Winter came and snow fell, and the children from Africa squealed and laughed in excitement and fear. They'd never seen anything like it before.

But for Afraa snow reminded her the mountains, of her Jiddoh, of Abdo Reeza, of Nadiha, of her lost home...It left bitter sweet memories, and then the snow too melted, and Afraa now was fluent in German, and so was little Yahya too. Baba quickly proved himself, his intelligence, and dedication, and was offered a job as a translator for the government, helping other new arriving families to settle, to find work, to fill out papers, to understand the trains and the taxis. Mama worked for the school, teaching again, as she had before Yahya was born. Abdo Yassin had gotten married, to a beautiful Indian lady with long black hair, who cooked very spicy food, and Afraa now had cousins. Family...It felt like roots shooting into the ground, holding her closer to this new place.

Slowly, it had started to feel like home. But she would never forget her birthplace, and whenever she visited the refugee welcoming center with Baba, she would sit with the children, and tell those tales of a Syria long ago. She shared stories of how the companions of the Prophet Muhammed (pbuh) had traveled to Syria, and how the Prophet himself had said that Syria was a blessed land. Stories of the Caliph Muawwiyah, Salahud din Ayubbi, the great and noble leaders. Stories of travelers who covered great distances to Syria, to visit, to study and learn, to appreciate her beauty. And her favorite stories that were about neighborhoods, filled with big families, laughing children, and especially the stories about two naughty little boys named Yousef and Reeza and how they would steal pomegranates from busy chaotic souks, and how their friendship spanned decades, and they eventually became old men who loved mint tea. Afraa spoke of a time when the air hung heavy with the scent of spices and smiles, not with gunpowder and fear. Most of these children had never known such a Syria, most of their parents had forgotten.

Baba always smiled when he heard her stories, and said she should write them down, so she could share them with Yahya, and Abdo Yassin's children one day. As always, Afraa nodded, but she knew as much as she loved this new home, Deutschland, she would never forget her birthplace, and every time she remembered it, she sent a quick prayer to the Heavens, that one day peace will again reign over the valleys and hills and through the towns and markets and every secret corner of the land.

Walking home that day Afraa stopped to look in the window of a bakery. The scent of cinnamon and pecan buns dancing in the breeze made her think of the great pistachio tree behind their house. Nadiha's brothers would climb the tree and collect bags of nuts for their mums. Nadiha and Afraa then helped their mums shell and roast the nuts and spice them in so many varieties. Sweet, salty, spicy, then they would slice some of the nuts, crush others, and even powder some of it. "Hey, buy something or move along," the shopkeeper yelled from the doorway. The welcoming tide of grace towards refugees and foreigners had long lost momentum. It had been replaced by distrust and anxiety and fear…Afraa nodded and continued on her way.

Afraa was always an eager learner and the same was true of her enthusiasm for language. She decided to learn English, to add to her already growing linguistic ability of Arabic, German and French. She started English lessons in the summer, and today she learnt a new word. Nostalgia. I know what it means now Afraa thought. Nostalgia is wanting to go home. Nostalgia is smelling the scent of Jasmine in the florist shop, and remembering the great bush of white flowers outside her parent's room window, that fragrance that danced in the night breeze, and carried with it the sweet possibility of hope. Nostalgia is remembering and missing and aching but do so with a smile on your heart.

Walking on Afraa thought to herself, years ago everyone smiled as we walked, but now people walk like broken souls inside stiff and inflexible bodies, eyes cold, mouth set in frown. When she was a child she beamed at everyone, friend and stranger. People stopped to say hello and shook hands, connected over glasses of tea and plates of sweet delights and wished God's blessings to one another. And the blessings themselves were so expressive, so heartfelt, so connecting that even through the new languages she was discovering, there wasn't much of a comparison to the depth of her poetic mother tongue. Ash-Shaam, land of beauty and family, land of history and culture, land of depth and poetry, land of knowledge and now land of scars. A land torn apart by a war which made its mothers cries, and fathers die, and its children scatter to foreign places like bags of rice flung out of the delivery vans at the refugee camps.

But the blood in her veins was Syrian, and the strength in her character was Syrian, and the determination to which she clung to was Syrian. Afraa never lost hope, and she never will. Syria will rise again, like the warrior who would not submit, like the jasmine after the winter, like the sunrise after a midnight storm.

Now Afraa ached but smiled as she remembered what Jiddoh always said, "The house of a tyrant is a ruin."

And then Abdo Reeza would take a sip of his tea and say,

"Tomorrow is close if you have patience."

Time would only tell…

Currents

Long after the setting of the golden orb
When the dark encloses
And the black blankets
The wind howls
And I wonder at the sounds
Carried through time
Are you singing of victories
Or do you ache with pain
Are you shouting joyously
Or do you cry with sadness
Tell me whirling swirling wind
Are you rousing us from our sleep
Are you calling us to action
Do you carry messages across the lands
Can you take my salaam to Aleppo and Homs?
Can you take my prayers to Gaza
Can you convey my solidarity to Myanmar
Can you tell the world we care
For if our leaders will stay deaf
We send our message with you
And if our leaders will be impotent
Tell them our Lord watches
And He will compensate
And tell them screaming shouting wind
That oppressors will never succeed
And for the oppressed eternal serenity awaits
Tell them wind that we haven't forgotten
We will never forget.

About the author:

In this debut novel by Ayesha Desai, we get to see her love and passion for things close to her heart.

She currently resides in Pretoria, South Africa with her husband and 2 young children. Ayesha is passionate about reading and this has evolved into a love of writing. Whilst this is her first published book, she has been writing for the last 20 years, and blogging since 2013.

She is a nature and outdoor enthusiast, but is equally happy baking at home with her children on a rainy day. Currently employed in the corporate sector, she still makes time to indulge her creative nature, by painting, and of course writing.

Her bucket list items include being able to travel more with her family, publishing an anthology of her poetry, seeing wild horses in the Namib desert, and eventually when her children are raised, retiring to a small town near the sea.

www.ingramcontent.com/pod-product-compliance
Lightning Source LLC
LaVergne TN
LVHW021123080426
835510LV00021B/3299